Preface

The art of embroidery as developed by The Danish Hand-craft Guild has spread far beyond the borders of Denmark itself. The subtle range of colours used and the way in which a sensitive observation of nature and slight stylization are harmoniously combined are two of the reasons why these beautiful designs are in demand throughout the world. Here in *Flower Designs in Cross-Stitch* we present a selection of patterns using birds, garlands and flowers that we hope will be enjoyed by the many people everywhere who are interested in embroidery.

A D E

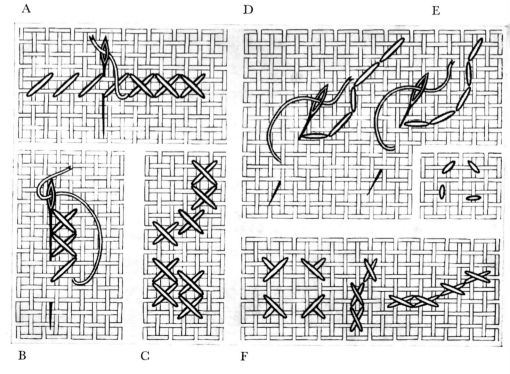

B C F

4

Method of working

A. Cross-stitches made in two journeys. All the under-stitches are sewn first, working from left to right. Each under-stitch is placed on the bias over 2 threads of material, going from the lower left-hand corner to the upper right-hand corner. To complete the cross-stitches, over-stitches are sewn in the opposite direction, working from right to left.

B. Cross-stitches sewn vertically. Each stitch is completed separately but the over-stitch still goes in the same direction as in figure A. The wrong side of both A and B will show only vertical stitches.

C. Cross-stitches worked in irregular sequence.

D. Two versions of backstitch used for details. On the left the two top backstitches go 2 threads sideways and 2 threads downwards; one stitch passes over 2 threads vertically and one stitch 2 threads horizontally. On the right the topmost backstitch passes over 2 threads downwards but only 1 thread sideways; and the fourth stitch passes over 2 threads sideways and 1 thread downwards. One vertical and one horizontal stitch are also shown.

E. (inset). Four backstitches each sewn over a single thread or over a single thread-cross.

F. On the left you can see four $\frac{3}{4}$ cross-stitches in which the under-stitch covers only 1 thread. In the middle and on the right you can see oblong cross-stitches which cover 1 thread in one direction and 2 threads in the other direction.

NB! The illustrations do not show the back of the cross-stitches.

Examples of cross-stitch work

With birds

Small mats

Linen type I.

Size: approx. 14.5 × 14.5 cm ($5\frac{3}{4}$ × $5\frac{3}{4}$ ins). Cutting measurements: 21 × 21 cm ($8\frac{3}{8}$ × $8\frac{3}{8}$ ins).

Measure 3 cm ($1\frac{1}{4}$ ins) inwards and downwards from the top left corner and start embroidering in the top left corner of the border. See drawing of pattern on page 8. Finally fold in the hem 3 threads from the embroidery. The hem has a width of 17 threads.

Cushion

Linen type II.

Size: approx. 34 × 34 cm ($13\frac{1}{2}$ × $13\frac{1}{2}$ ins). Cutting measurements: 40 × 40 cm (16 × 16 ins).

Measure 6 cm ($2\frac{3}{8}$ ins) inwards and downwards from the top left corner and start embroidering in the top left corner of the cushion's border. See drawing of pattern on page 8.

When the border has been worked, find the centre of the cushion and of the pattern and start embroidering the bird motif from there.

Wall hanging

Linen type II.

Size: approx. 30 × 75 cm (12 × 30 ins). Cutting measurements: 43 × 90 cm ($17\frac{1}{4}$ × 36 ins).

The wall hanging illustrated here has the bird motifs shown on pages 37, 51 and 31, surrounded by a green border (No. 40 light green).

Measure 9 cm ($3\frac{5}{8}$ ins) inwards and downwards from the top left corner and start embroidering the top left corner of the green border. This border is the same as on the small mats. See drawing of pattern on page 8.

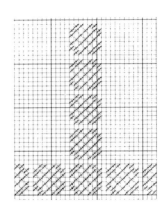

On the left is shown the drawing of the pattern for the cushion's border. On the right the border for the wall hanging.

Finish the work by folding in the hem 2·5 cm (1 in) from the embroidery. Sew down the hems, leaving the top and bottom ones open at the sides. Pull a narrow tape through the top and bottom hem and close the seams. Two small brass rings can be attached to the back of the upper hem for hanging.

With flowers

Small mat

Linen type I.

Size: 16 × 16 cm (6⅜ × 6⅜ ins). Cutting measurements: 21 × 21 cm (8⅜ × 8⅜ ins).

Find the centre of the material and of the motif and start the embroidering from there. The hem has a width of 8 threads with a hemstitch over 3 threads.

Cushion

Linen type I.

Size: 30 × 30 cm (12 × 12 ins). Cutting measurements: 35 × 70 cm (14 × 28 ins).

The colours for the border are No. 40 (light green) at the outside and No. 100 (medium green) innermost. The material is divided in two equal parts. Start with the border 7 cm (2¾ ins) inwards and downwards in the top left corner. The middle of the border is marked on the drawing on page 11 with a dotted line. When the border is finished, pinpoint the centre of the cushion and the centre of the motif. The embroidering of the motif starts from this point.

Tray cloth

Linen type I.

Size: 43 × 32 cm (17¼ × 12¾ ins). Cutting measurements: 48 × 38 cm (19 × 15 ins).

Start with the edging as in the drawing on page 10, colour No. 10 (light green), 2·5 cm (1 in) inwards and downwards in top left corner. The edging covers 502 threads on the long side and 382 threads on the short, which equals 251 × 191 stitches. The distance from the border to the extreme edge of the motif is 10 threads upwards and 10 threads sideways. The hem has a width of 8 threads and is sewn up to the edging in the normal way.

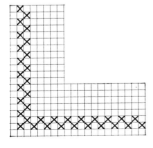

On the left is a drawing of the pattern for a tray cloth border. On the right the cushion and a drawing of patterns for the cushion's border.

12

With garlands

Small mat

Linen type I.

Size: approx. 15.5 × 15.5 cm ($6\frac{1}{4}$ × $6\frac{1}{4}$ ins). Cutting measurements: 21 × 21 cm ($8\frac{3}{8}$ × $8\frac{3}{8}$ ins).

Find the centre of the material, which is also the centre of the motif. Follow the middle line from the centre out to the nearest leaf or flower and start the embroidering from there.

The hem has a width of 8 threads with a hemstitch over 3 threads.

Runner

Linen type I.

Size: approx. 18 × 136 cm ($7\frac{1}{4}$ × 54 ins). Cutting measurements: 25 × 145 cm (10 × 58 ins).

The runner has 9 garlands. Start with the middle one and work as for the small mat.

The distance between each garland should be 14.5 cm ($5\frac{3}{4}$ ins) measured from centre to centre.

Finally fold in the hem at a distance of 3 cm ($1\frac{1}{4}$ in) from the edge of the garlands on all sides of the runner. The hem has a width of 8 threads with a hemstitch over 3 threads.

Cushion

Linen type II.

Size: approx. 33 × 33 cm (13 × 13 ins). Cutting measurements: 41 × 41 cm ($16\frac{3}{8}$ × $16\frac{3}{8}$ ins).

The method of working is the same as for the small mat. Mount the cushion with a trimming ribbon in a colour to match the motif.

Square tray cloth

Linen type II.

Size: approx. 26.5 × 26.5 cm $(10\frac{5}{8} \times 10\frac{5}{8}$ ins). Cutting measurements: 34 × 34 cm $(13\frac{5}{8} \times 13\frac{5}{8}$ ins).

The method of working is the same as for the small mat. The hem has a width of 7 threads with a hemstitch over 3 threads.

The garland motif can be decorated particularly well with lettering, a name or a year for example. If sewn on linen type I it is best to use letters covering 5 stitches. On linen type II letters covering 7 stitches are better. (See *A Handbook of Lettering for Stitchers* by Elsie Svennas).

Material and instructions

The designs in this book are useful for small mats, runners, cushions, wall hangings, table cloths and tray cloths.

The embroideries are made either on a fine evenweave linen with a thread density of 12 threads per cm, approx. 30 threads per inch (in this book called type I) or on a coarse evenweave linen with a thread density of 7 threads per cm, approx. 18 threads per inch (type II).

On linen I you should sew with 1 thread Danish Flower Thread or with 4 strands of stranded cotton using a tapestry needle No. 24 or 26.

On canvas II you should sew with 2 threads Danish Flower Thread or with 4 strands of stranded cotton using a tapestry needle No. 22.

On each design chart there are 4 arrows showing the central lines in the motif. The centre of the motif is found at the point where these lines intersect.

A square in the pattern equals 2 threads in the canvas.

All designs in the book should be worked with the Flower Thread supplied by *The Danish Handcraft Guild, 38 Vimmelskaftet, 1161 Copenhagen K, Denmark,* who will send a shade card on request. The shade numbers quoted refer to these threads, which are made of very fine lustreless cotton yarn in delicate natural colours. DMC or mouliné (stranded cotton) is also used for some white areas.

If not obtainable locally, Danish Evenweave Linens, Flower Threads, and DMC mouliné (stranded cotton) may be obtained from Mace and Nairn, 89 Crane Street, Salisbury, Wiltshire, England. When ordering the linens, refer to type I as linen II and type II as linen D.

Washing and ironing instructions

Danish Flower Thread is dyed with the best and truest dyes that can be manufactured and to keep the colours bright, articles on which it is used should be washed and ironed very carefully.

Washing. The embroidery must be rinsed in cold water, washed by hand in cold or lukewarm water with soap flakes, then rinsed again in cold water, before being laid to dry between two white cloths.

Ironing. The embroidery should be laid with the right side down on a soft under-cloth and a piece of thin material should be placed over it. It is then ironed until the material is dry.

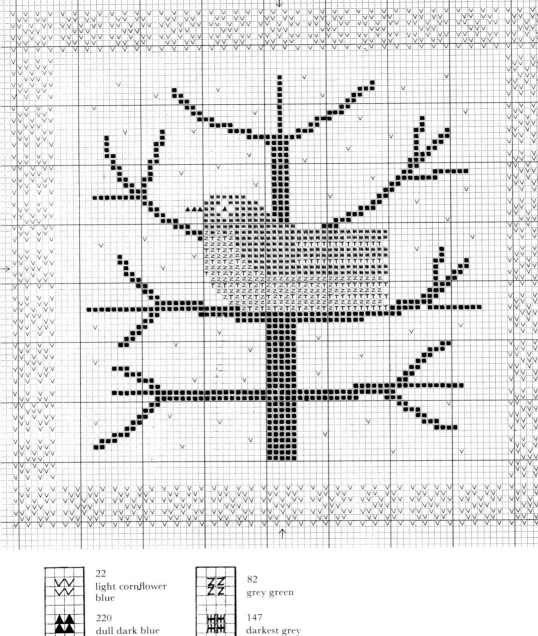

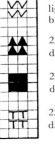

22
light cornflower
blue

220
dull dark blue

201
dark blue

226
dark turquoise

82
grey green

147
darkest grey

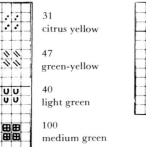

	31 citrus yellow		213 medium brown		213 medium brown
	47 green-yellow		26 yellow-green		
	40 light green		210 deep dark green		
	100 medium green				

Winter Jasmine
Jasminum nudiflorum

19

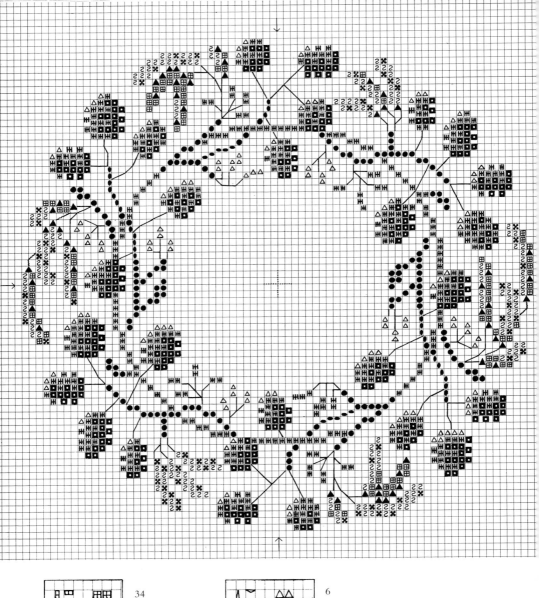

34 dark yellow-green		6 dark gold-yellow
212 olive green		216 deep dark brown
26 yellow-green		206 dark olive green
215 soil colour		240 black

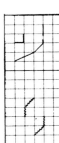

216
deep dark brown

206
dark olive green

Alder
Alnus glutinosa

21

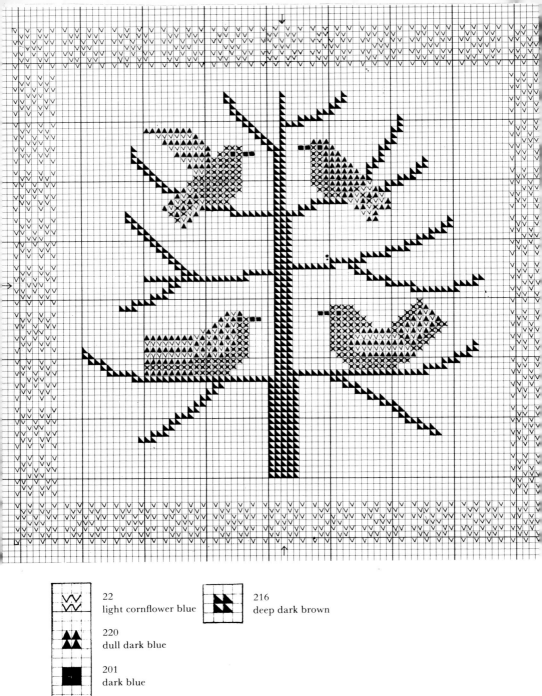

	22		216
	light cornflower blue		deep dark brown

220
dull dark blue

201
dark blue

23
lavender blue

23

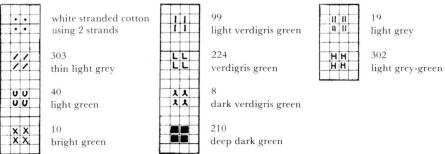

· · / · / ·	white stranded cotton using 2 strands	
/ / / /	303 thin light grey	
∪ ∪ ∪ ∪	40 light green	
X X X X	10 bright green	
‖ ‖ ‖ ‖	99 light verdigris green	
L L L L	224 verdigris green	
⅄ ⅄ ⅄ ⅄	8 dark verdigris green	
■ ■ ■ ■	210 deep dark green	
‖ ‖ ‖ ‖	19 light grey	
H H H H	302 light grey-green	

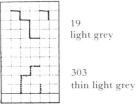

19
light grey

303
thin light grey

Snowdrop
Galanthus nivalis

25

223		dull light green
5		mauve
10		bright green
40		light green
100		medium green
215		soil colour
6		dark gold-yellow
210		deep dark green
27		light mauve

Sweet Violet
Viola odorata

27

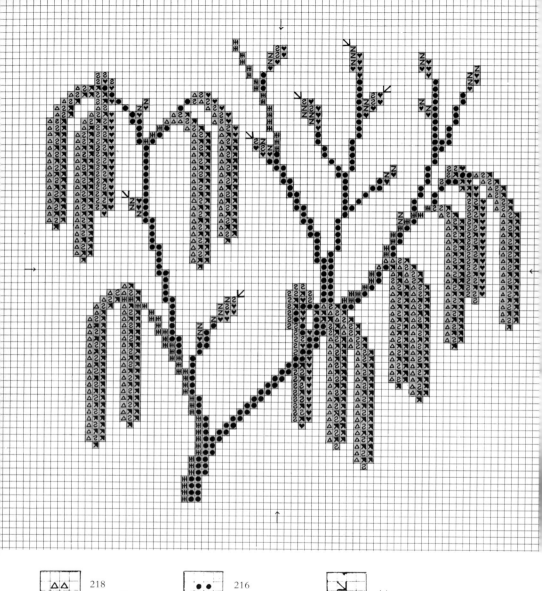

	218
△△ / △△	grey-yellow
	26
ς ς / ς ς	yellow-green
	6
✖	dark gold-yellow
	212
♥♥	olive green

	216
•• / ••	deep dark brown
	213
Ƶ Ƶ / Ƶ Ƶ	medium brown
	215
H H H / H H H	soil colour

	14
↘ / ↖	dark brick red

Hazel
Corylus avellana
29

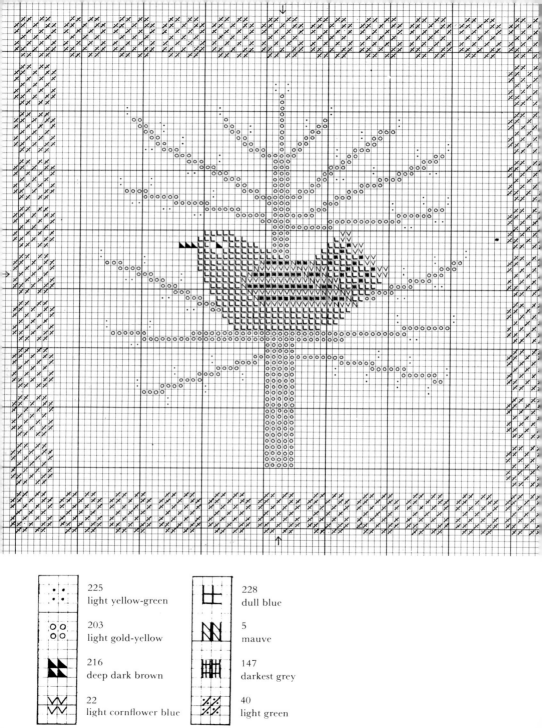

	225		228
	light yellow-green		dull blue
	203		5
	light gold-yellow		mauve
	216		147
	deep dark brown		darkest grey
	22		40
	light cornflower blue		light green

48 yellow	224 verdigris green	26 yellow-green
31 lemon yellow	210 deep dark green	8 dark verdigris green
47 green-yellow	34 dark yellow-green	99 light verdigris green
225 light yellow-green	222 beige	53 orange-yellow

Wild Daffodil
Narcissus pseudonarcissus

33

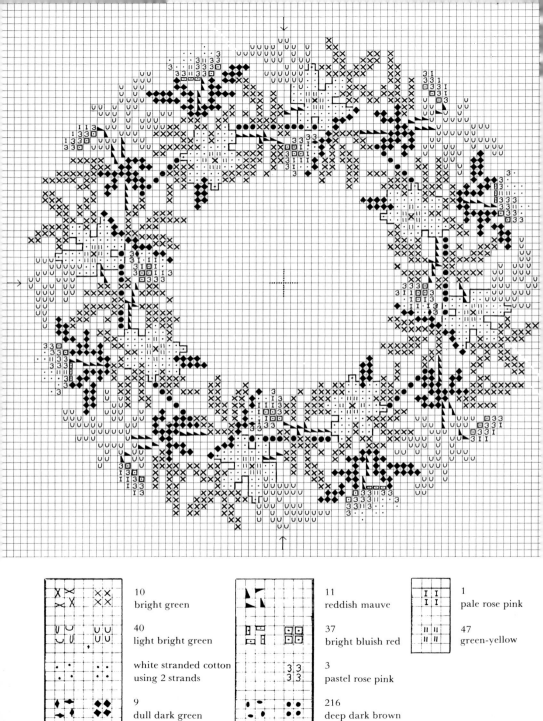

	10 bright green
	40 light bright green
	white stranded cotton using 2 strands
	9 dull dark green

	11 reddish mauve
	37 bright bluish red
	3 pastel rose pink
	216 deep dark brown

	1 pale rose pink
	47 green-yellow

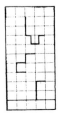

27
light mauve

Wood Anemone
Anemone nemorosa

35

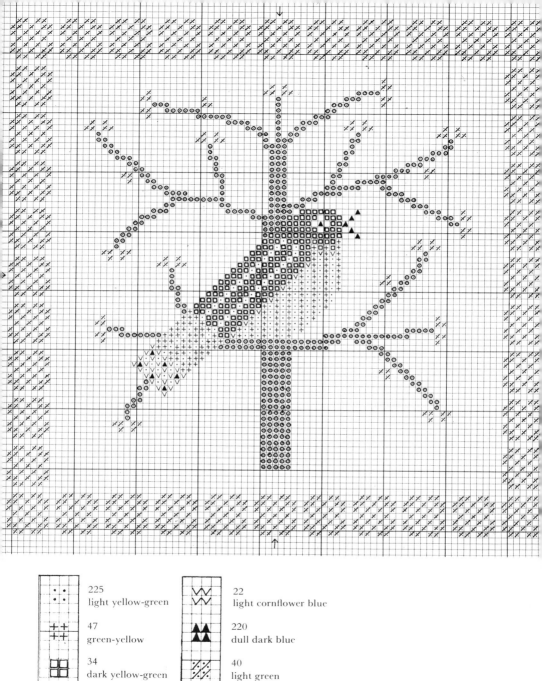

· · / · ·	225 light yellow-green	W W / W W	22 light cornflower blue
+ + / + +	47 green-yellow	▲▲ / ▲▲	220 dull dark blue
⊞ / ⊞	34 dark yellow-green	⁄ ⁄ / ⁄ ⁄	40 light green
⊙⊙ / ⊙⊙	215 soil colour		

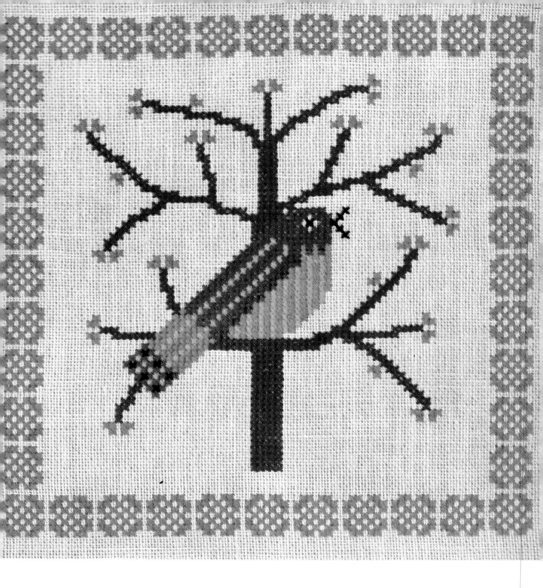

U U / U U	40 light green	
Q Q / Q Q	100 medium green	
H H / H H	215 soil colour	
Λ Λ / Δ Δ	6 dark gold-yellow	
+ + / + +	505 bright yellow-green	
⌐ ⌐ / ⌐ ⌐	101 bright green	
– – / – –	225 light yellow-green	
▢ ▢ / ▢ ▢	203 light gold-yellow	
Z Z / Z Z	213 medium brown	
▲▲ / ▲▲	206 dark olive green	

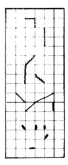

223
dull light green

213
medium brown

40
light green

206
dark olive green

101
bright green

Beech
Fagus sylvatica
39

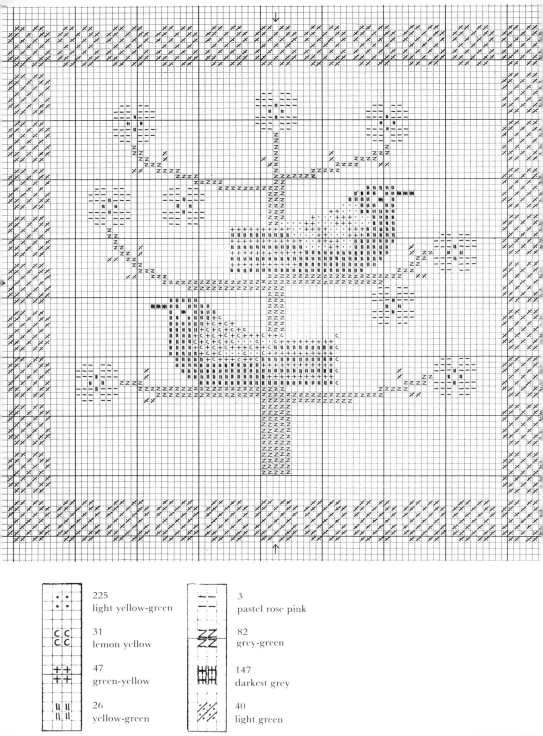

	225 light yellow-green
	3 pastel rose pink
	31 lemon yellow
	82 grey-green
	47 green-yellow
	147 darkest grey
	26 yellow-green
	40 light green

41

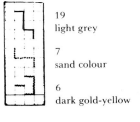

19
light grey

7
sand colour

6
dark gold-yellow

Pheasant's Eye Narcissus
Narcissus poeticus

43

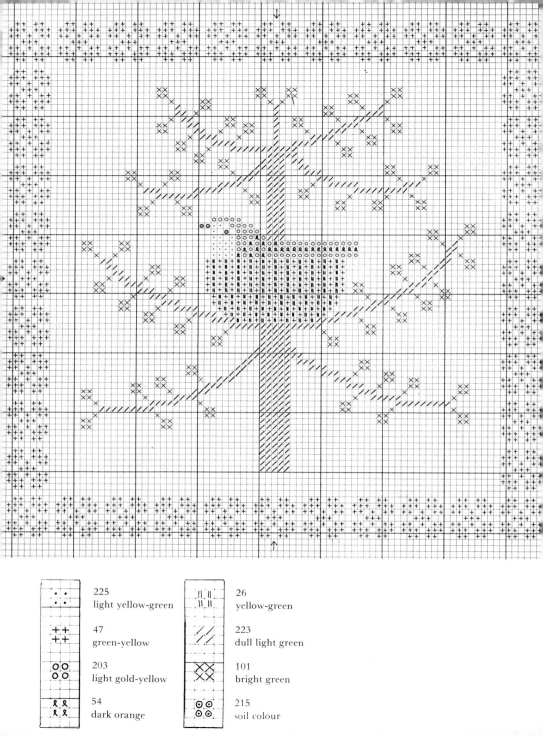

	225 light yellow-green		26 yellow-green
	47 green-yellow		223 dull light green
	203 light gold-yellow		101 bright green
	54 dark orange		215 soil colour

45

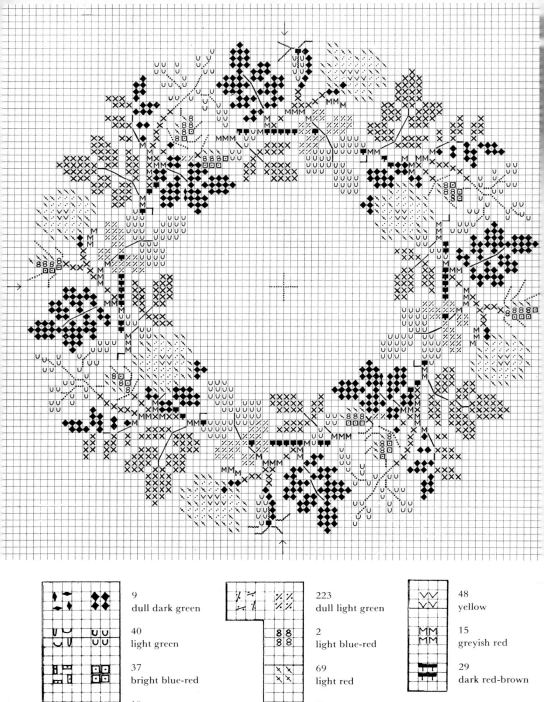

			9 dull dark green
	40 light green
	37 bright blue-red
	10 bright green

	223 dull light green
	2 light blue-red
	69 light red
	0 white

	48 yellow
	15 greyish red
	29 dark red-brown

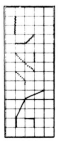

29
dark red-brown

10
bright green

15
greyish red

Dog Rose
Rosa canina

47

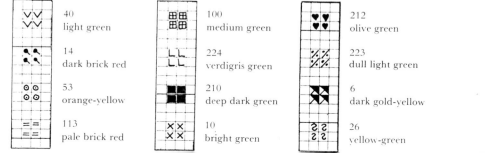

	40 light green		100 medium green		212 olive green
	14 dark brick red		224 verdigris green		223 dull light green
	53 orange-yellow		210 deep dark green		6 dark gold-yellow
	113 pale brick red		10 bright green		26 yellow-green

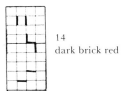

14
dark brick red

French Marigold
Tagetes patula nana
49

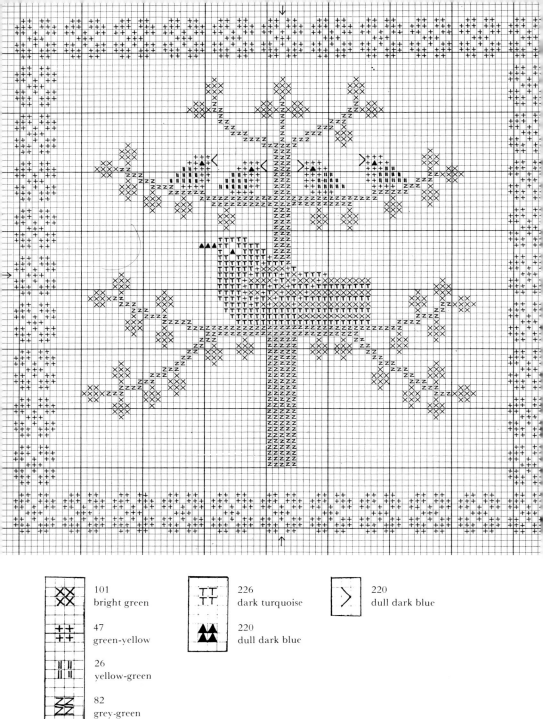

	101 bright green			226 dark turquoise			220 dull dark blue
	47 green-yellow			220 dull dark blue			
	26 yellow-green						
	82 grey-green						

210 deep dark green	10 bright green	86 bright red
100 medium green	40 light green	93 light carrot
5 mauve	47 green-yellow	206 dark olive green
223 dull light green	101 bright green	97 dark red

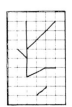

100
medium green

Bittersweet
Solanum dulcamara

53

Symbol	Number	Name
	100	medium green
	10	bright green
	223	dull light green
	47	green-yellow
	31	lemon yellow
	210	deep dark green
	15	greyish red
	6	dark gold-yellow
	203	light gold-yellow
	34	dark yellow-green
	9	dull dark green

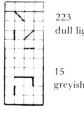

223
dull light green

15
greyish red

Rose
Rosa hybrida

55

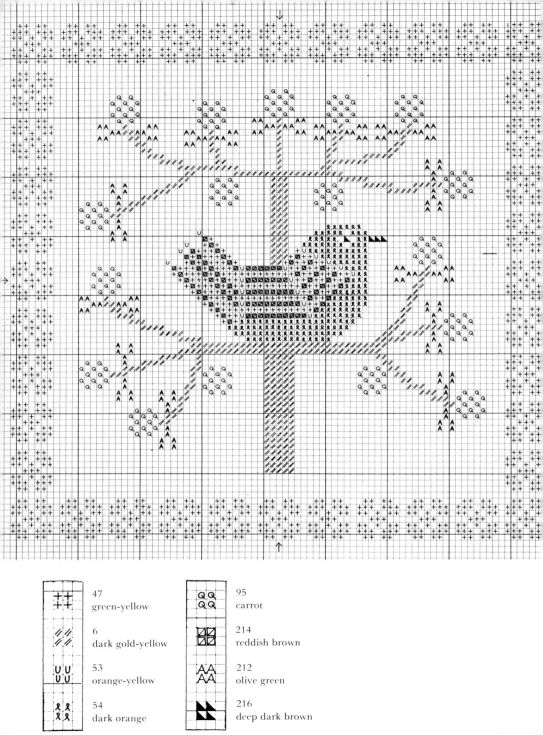

++ ++	**47** green-yellow	
// //	**6** dark gold-yellow	
U U U U	**53** orange-yellow	
⅄⅄ ⅄⅄	**54** dark orange	

Q Q Q Q	**95** carrot	
▨▨ ▨▨	**214** reddish brown	
AA AA	**212** olive green	
◣◥ ◥◣	**216** deep dark brown	

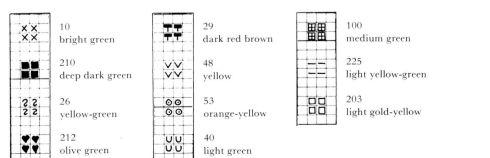

✕✕ / ✕✕ 10 bright green	T T / T T 29 dark red brown	⊞⊞ / ⊞⊞ 100 medium green
■ 210 deep dark green	V V / V V 48 yellow	— — / — — 225 light yellow-green
2 2 / 2 2 26 yellow-green	◯◯ / ◯◯ 53 orange-yellow	▢▢ / ▢▢ 203 light gold-yellow
♥ ♥ / ♥ ♥ 212 olive green	U U / U U 40 light green	

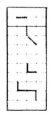

26
yellow-green

29
dark red brown

Ligularia
Senecio clivorum

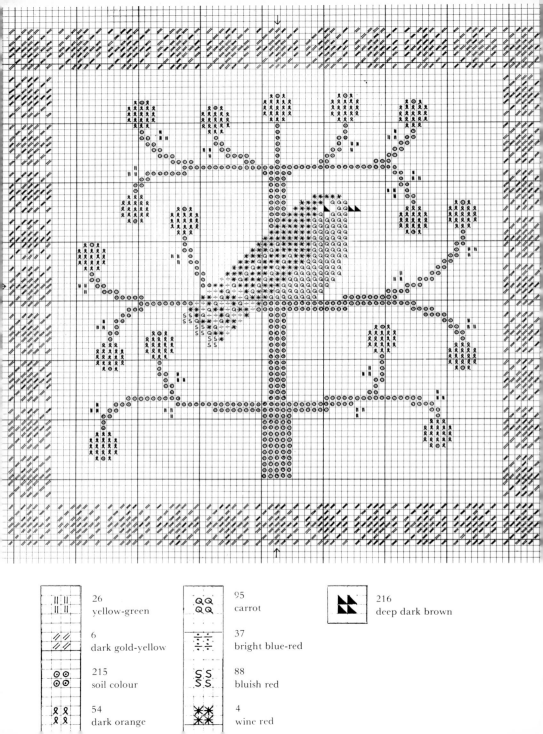

26 yellow-green	**95** carrot	**216** deep dark brown
6 dark gold-yellow	**37** bright blue-red	
215 soil colour	**88** bluish red	
54 dark orange	**4** wine red	

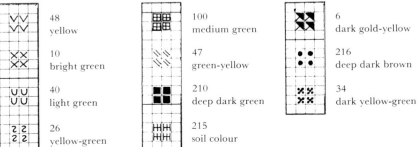

	48 yellow		100 medium green		6 dark gold-yellow
	10 bright green		47 green-yellow		216 deep dark brown
	40 light green		210 deep dark green		34 dark yellow-green
	26 yellow-green		215 soil colour		

Helenium
Helenium hybridum

63

△ ▲	△△	6	*783*
▲ △	△△	dark gold-yellow	

✕ ⋉	✕✕	212 *469 734*
⋊ ✕	✕✕	olive green

2 ≈	2 2	2 *734 469*
≈ 2	2 2	light blue-red

⊖ ⊙	⊙⊙	96
⊖ ⊙	⊙⊙	brick red *922*

◩ ◪	◪◪	4
◪ ◩	◪◪	wine red *918*

E ◄		113 *Dmc 402*
E E	E E	pale brick red

◉ ◉	◉◉	14
◉ ◉	◉◉	dark brick red *920*

212
olive green

Virginia Creeper
Parthenocissus quinquefolia

65

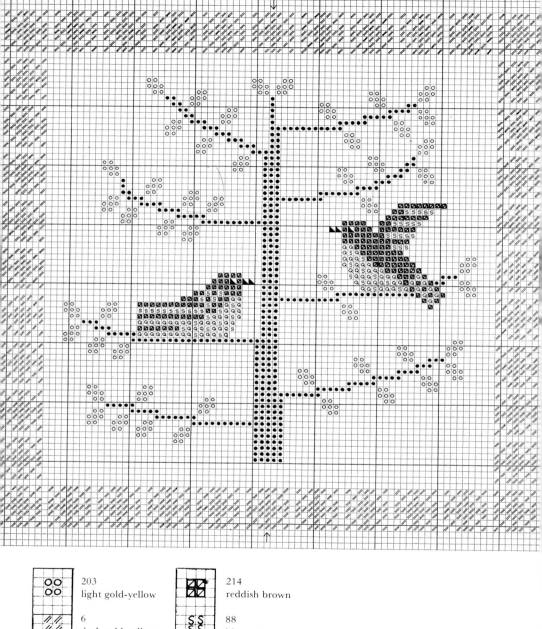

	203 light gold-yellow		214 reddish brown
	6 dark gold-yellow		88 blue-red
	216 deep dark brown		206 dark olive green
	95 carrot		

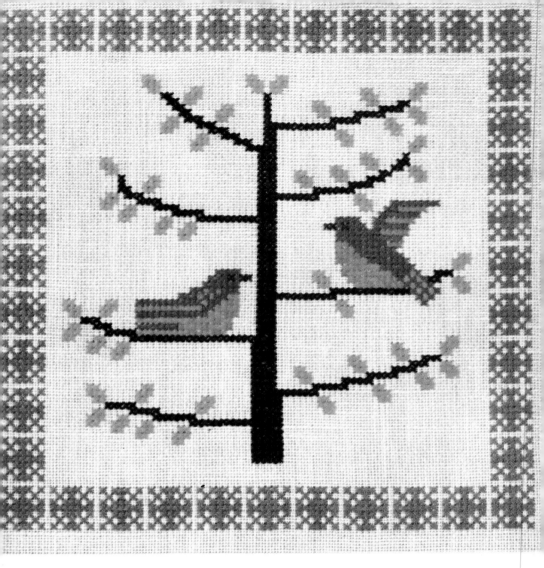

	82 grey-green		225 light yellow-green		4 wine red
	223 dull light green		26 yellow-green		
	47 green-yellow		100 medium green		
	6 dark gold-yellow		212 olive green		

82
grey-green

Lime
Tilia cordata

69

VV VV	22 light cornflower blue
▲▲	220 dull dark blue
✖	23 lavender blue
⫽⫽	6 dark gold-yellow

◸◹	216 deep dark brown
⊞⊞⊞	147 darkest grey

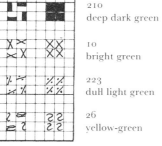	210	deep dark green
	10	bright green
	223	dull light green
	26	yellow-green

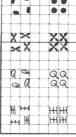	216	deep dark brown
	212	olive green
	100	medium green
	215	soil colour

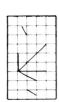

212
olive green

Ivy
Hedera helix
73

100 medium green	93 light carrot	34 dark yellow-green
48 yellow	10 bright green	9 dull dark green
203 light gold-yellow	14 dark brick red	
210 deep dark green	206 dark olive green	

206
dark olive green

Chrysanthemum
Chrysanthemum indicum

75

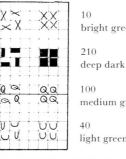

10
bright green

210
deep dark green

100
medium green

40
light green

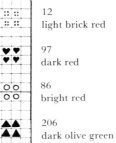

12
light brick red

97
dark red

86
bright red

206
dark olive green

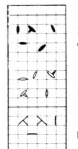

210
deep dark green

100
medium green

10
bright green

40
light green

206
dark olive green

Holly
Ilex aquifolium

77

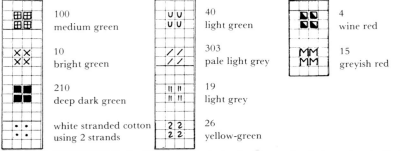

100 medium green	40 light green	4 wine red
10 bright green	303 pale light grey	15 greyish red
210 deep dark green	19 light grey	
white stranded cotton using 2 strands	26 yellow-green	

Christmas Rose
Helleborus niger

79